Georgia Supervised Visitation Training Manual

First Edition – August 2025

For permission requests, contact:

Dr. Arkeria S. Wright Publishing Company, LLC.
Email: dr.arkeriaswrightpublishingco@gmail.com
Website: www.thechildrensadvocate.com

DR. ARKERIA S. WRIGHT

Published in the United States of America.
ISBN: 979-8-9997813-0-7

Georgia Supervised Visitation Training Manual

Published for The Children's Advocate, LLC
Prepared by Dr. Arkeria S. Wright
Incorporating Georgia DFCS policy guidance and state law on supervised visitation

Date: August 2025

Disclaimer

This training manual is designed to provide guidance for both private supervised visitation providers and professionals working with Georgia's Division of Family & Children Services (DFCS). While it references Georgia law, court standards, and DFCS policies, it is not a substitute for legal counsel or state-issued licensing requirements. This manual is independently authored and is not affiliated with or endorsed by DFCS or the Georgia Department of Human Services. Always consult your local court orders and agency guidelines.

Acknowledgments

Special thanks to the many providers, child welfare professionals, and court officers who support the reunification of families across Georgia and those that advocate for children with love. This manual would not have been possible without the dedication of those working in both public and private roles to ensure safe, meaningful contact between children and their parents.

Dedication

To my children,

Ashalah and Amari, who are my greatest teachers, my deepest inspiration, and my constant reminder of why this work matters. You have shown me the beauty of resilience, the power of love, and the importance of creating safe spaces where children can simply be children.

And to every child whose life has crossed my path in classrooms, courtrooms, visitation and community spaces, you are the heartbeat of this mission. Your stories, your courage, and your voices have shaped this work more than any law or training ever could.

May this manual stand as a small part of a much greater effort to ensure that every child is seen, heard, and protected, and that those entrusted with their care are equipped to honor the sacred trust placed in them.

With love and unwavering hope

Table of Contents

Chapter 1: Introduction & Purpose

Dear Advocate,

Welcome to the Georgia Supervised Visitation Training Manual. Whether you are a professional working within the child welfare system or an entrepreneur establishing a private practice, your commitment to ensuring the safety, well-being, and family connection of children in high-conflict custody situations is critical. It is an act of love.

The goal of this manual is to equip you with the knowledge, legal foundation, and best practices necessary to provide safe, effective, and trauma-informed supervised visitation services. In Georgia, supervised visitation providers operate across a diverse spectrum: some work directly under DFCS policy and court mandate, while others function as independent practitioners, contracted by attorneys, families, or court orders.

This guide is especially valuable for those starting or expanding a private practice, as it demystifies the expectations, documentation procedures, safety protocols, and legal obligations that govern this space. Whether you are a social worker, therapist, educator, or professional seeking to serve families with care and neutrality, this manual will serve as both a foundational training tool and a continuing reference.

Thank you for choosing to support families in transition. Your role is vital. Your love is imperative.

Sincerely,

Dr. Arkeria S. Wright Founder, The Children's Advocate

1.2 Definition of Supervised Visitation

Supervised visitation is a form of court-ordered or agency-mandated contact between a parent (or other party) and a child, during which an approved third-party supervisor is present to monitor, observe, and document the interaction. The purpose of supervision is to ensure the safety and emotional well-being of the child while maintaining the relationship with the parent in a structured, controlled setting. The supervisor may be required to intervene, redirect, or end the visit if safety is compromised.

Definition of a Supervised Visitation Program

A supervised visitation program refers to the structured operation or entity —either public or private—that offers, manages, or facilitates these supervised interactions between a child and a non-custodial parent or family member. These programs may function through DFCS contracts, juvenile court mandates, nonprofit organizations, or independent private practice. All programs should adhere to policies, safety standards, reporting obligations, and training guidelines that align with Georgia law and the best interest of the child.

Chapter 1.3: Types of Supervised Visitation

Supervised visitation can take multiple forms depending on the circumstances of the case, the court's order, and the provider's structure:

1. **Monitored Visitation (Non-Interventionist)**
   - Supervisor is present and observing but does not interact unless necessary for safety or clarity.
   - Typically used when risks are moderate or visitation has been ongoing without incident.
2. **Therapeutic Supervised Visitation**
   - Conducted by a licensed therapist or clinical social worker.
   - Includes assessment, support, and sometimes guided interaction for reunification or behavioral change.
3. **Fully Structured Supervision (Interventionist)**
   - Supervisor actively monitors, redirects, and structures interaction as needed.
   - Appropriate for high-conflict cases or where a parent needs specific behavioral coaching.
4. **Group Supervised Visitation**
   - Multiple families share a space with multiple supervisors, often used in agency settings.
   - Cost-effective but less individualized; not suitable for high-risk cases.
5. **Virtual Supervised Visitation**
   - Conducted via video conferencing tools when in-person contact is impossible or inappropriate.
   - Must include safety protocols and be court-approved.
6. **Exchange Monitoring or Supervised Transfer**
   - Supervisor oversees only the hand-off of the child between parents, ensuring no direct contact or conflict.

Common Reasons for Supervised Visitation

Courts order supervised visitation for a variety of reasons intended to protect the child while preserving the parent-child relationship:

- **Allegations or History of Abuse or Neglect**
  To protect the child from physical, sexual, or emotional harm while allowing the parent to demonstrate progress.

- **Domestic Violence Involving One or Both Parents**
  To prevent exposure to violence and minimize fear or manipulation during visitation.

- **Substance Use or Mental Health Concerns**
  When a parent is actively in treatment or has a recent history of instability.

- **High-Conflict Custody Cases**
  Where communication between parties is severely strained and could impact the child.

- **Reunification Cases through DFCS**
  Often used as a transition step when a child has been in foster care and contact is being reestablished with a parent.

- **Court Sanctions or Protective Orders**
  When a parent is under restraining orders, probation, or has a restricted parenting plan.

- **Failure to Follow Parenting Plans or Court Orders**
  As a remedial step for parents who have not complied with past visitation agreements.

1.4 Why Theory and Research Matter in Supervised Visitation

Supervised visitation is not merely logistical—it is a high-stakes, child-centered intervention grounded in psychology, law, and systems theory. Expert providers must move beyond observation and into intentional, informed practice. Understanding the theoretical underpinnings of child development, family systems, and trauma response allows supervisors to better interpret behavior, maintain neutrality, and serve as credible reporters to the court.

This section outlines the most critical theories informing supervised visitation and why every provider should integrate research-based insight into their daily work.

Attachment Theory (Bowlby, Ainsworth)

Attachment theory asserts that children form emotional bonds with caregivers beginning in infancy, which impact their sense of safety, trust, and future relationships. In cases involving removal from the home, separation, or trauma, these attachments may be disrupted.

For supervisors, understanding secure versus insecure attachments helps in:

- Interpreting a child's emotional responses during transitions
- Identifying behavioral cues (clinging, withdrawal, regression)
- Evaluating whether the parent is sensitive to the child's attachment needs

🧠 ***Example:*** A child who avoids eye contact or flinches during hugs may be displaying avoidant attachment responses—not simply "being shy." A trained supervisor will document such patterns objectively, potentially informing therapeutic referrals or parenting interventions.

Trauma-Informed Care (SAMHSA Framework)

Trauma-informed supervision acknowledges that children in supervised visitation often have histories of:

- Domestic violence exposure
- Sexual abuse or neglect
- Parental mental illness or substance use
- Involvement in the foster care system

A trauma-informed approach encourages supervisors to:

- Recognize trauma triggers (tone of voice, gestures, location)
- Create safe, predictable routines
- Avoid re-traumatization during transitions or observations

This lens is particularly vital when writing reports or determining the pacing of step-down transitions. Even progress must be managed sensitively when trauma is present.

Family Systems Theory

Family systems theory (Bowen, 1978) views each individual as part of a larger relational system. Behavior cannot be assessed in isolation—every member of the family influences the emotional climate.

In supervised visitation, this theory encourages providers to:

- Observe family interaction patterns (enmeshment, triangulation, detachment)
- Stay alert to boundary testing or role reversal
- Maintain neutrality in high-conflict co-parenting dynamics

🧠 ***Example***: A child acting out in visits may be reacting not to the parent, but to the stress of conflict between adults. Supervisors trained in systems thinking avoid over-attributing causality.

Observational Objectivity & Bias Awareness

Cognitive psychology highlights how bias affects perception—even among trained professionals. Supervisors must continually self-monitor:

- Confirmation bias (expecting to see bad behavior)
- Halo effect (being overly influenced by one positive or negative incident)
- Cultural bias (misinterpreting parenting through a majority lens)

The use of consistent observation tools, checklists, and documentation standards is not simply a best practice—it is an ethical requirement for neutrality.

Why This Matters in Practice

Understanding theory enables supervisors to:

- Write stronger, more contextualized visit reports
- Prevent misinterpretation of child behavior
- Avoid unintentional favoritism or advocacy
- Collaborate more effectively with therapists, case managers, and attorneys
- Build credibility with judges and the legal system

Supervised visitation is not "babysitting." It is trauma-sensitive, court-involved social intervention that requires informed, professional decision-making at every stage. Theory gives supervisors the lens to do this work with precision, compassion, and reliability.

1.5 The Role of Cultural Responsiveness in Supervised Visitation

Cultural responsiveness is the capacity of a visitation provider to recognize, respect, and adapt to the diverse backgrounds, beliefs, and parenting norms of the families they serve. Families engaged in supervised visitation often come from marginalized communities, and their interactions with the child welfare or legal system are deeply influenced by race, ethnicity, religion, socioeconomic status, immigration status, and language.

Supervisors must avoid the assumption that **all parenting practices fit a universal mold**. A culturally responsive provider asks:

- Is what I'm observing unsafe, or just unfamiliar?
- Am I interpreting behavior through my own cultural lens?
- Am I documenting in a way that respects difference while protecting safety?

Cultural Competence vs. Cultural Humility

While cultural competence refers to understanding diverse groups, cultural humility emphasizes ongoing self-awareness and the understanding that no provider is ever fully "done" learning. This mindset is crucial in maintaining neutrality and avoiding bias in observation and reporting.

Implications for Supervised Visitation

Culturally responsive supervision includes:

- Avoiding mislabeling extended family involvement as "over-involvement" or chaos
- Recognizing the role of religion, dress, or gender expectations in parenting
- Using interpreters when needed and avoiding assumptions about language comprehension
- Acknowledging historical trauma and distrust in court systems (especially for BIPOC families)

Documentation Example:

❌ Poor: "Father refused to look child in the eye or show emotion."

☑️ Better: "Father maintained a calm tone and minimal direct eye contact; this may reflect cultural norms around emotional expression or authority."

Why It Matters

Without cultural responsiveness, supervised visitation becomes a place where difference is penalized. With it, it becomes a space of safety, dignity, and respect—without compromising the child's best interests. Providers who lead with empathy and humility become trusted figures in an often adversarial system.

Chapter 2: Legal Framework in Georgia

Introduction

Supervised visitation providers in Georgia operate within a clearly defined legal environment that protects the rights and safety of children and families. Whether working through the Division of Family & Children Services (DFCS) or in private practice, supervisors must be familiar with the state statutes, court orders, and agency policies that govern their role. A strong understanding of the legal framework ensures that providers not only remain compliant but also maintain credibility with the courts, attorneys, and clients they serve. This chapter outlines the primary Georgia laws, DFCS guidelines, and judicial considerations that shape supervised visitation, offering a foundation for ethical, effective, and legally sound practice.

2.1 Georgia Code §19-9-7 — Visitation in Cases Involving Family Violence or Risk

Under Georgia law, O.C.G.A. §19-9-7 outlines specific conditions under which a court may allow visitation—even when there is a history of family violence, substance abuse, or significant risk to the child or custodial party. Supervised visitation is often ordered when the court finds it necessary to protect the safety and welfare of the child and any victim of domestic violence.

Judges have broad discretion to impose any of the following conditions on the visiting parent:

- Mandatory supervision by a neutral third party.
- Completion of a certified Family Violence Intervention Program (FVIP).
- Prohibition against the use of alcohol or controlled substances within 24 hours before or during the visit.
- Payment of costs related to supervised visitation.
- Restrictions against overnight visits or unsupervised contact.
- Issuance of protective orders.
- Requirement to post a bond or provide proof of rehabilitation.
- Confidentiality protections for the child's and victim's residential or school addresses.

The statute also explicitly permits courts to deny visitation altogether if no condition can guarantee the child's safety.

Relevance for Providers:

- Private providers should review court orders carefully to ensure compliance with imposed restrictions (e.g., location, supervision level, substance testing).
- DFCS case managers must document such court-ordered restrictions in SHINES and ensure that caregivers and facility staff are informed and trained to follow the court's instructions precisely.

2.2 Georgia Code §19-9-3 — Best Interest of the Child

Georgia's general custody and visitation statute, O.C.G.A. §19-9-3, requires courts to determine visitation based solely on what is in the best interest of the child. The law lists more than a dozen factors the court may consider when making custody and visitation decisions, including:

- The emotional ties between each parent and the child.
- The ability of each parent to provide for the child's basic needs and education.
- The home environment of each parent.
- The mental and physical health of all parties involved.
- The criminal history, if any, of each parent.
- Any evidence of family violence, neglect, or substance abuse.
- The child's wishes (especially if the child is 11 or older, with formal consideration at 14+).

This statute serves as the foundation for visitation planning in Georgia, and both DFCS and private supervisors should understand how their documentation may ultimately support or inform judicial decisions regarding custody and future parenting time.

Relevance for Providers:

DFCS staff must evaluate visitation through the lens of reunification goals, safety, and the family's progression toward permanency.
Private providers must document facts objectively, noting patterns that reflect or contradict the child's best interests (e.g., parental engagement, boundary-setting, emotional safety).

The definitions, types, and reasons provide a solid foundation to understand why Georgia law (O.C.G.A. §19-9-7 and §19-9-3) places such importance on safety, structure, and discretion in crafting visitation conditions.

Chapter 3: DFCS Guidelines & Policies – Application to Private Practice

Introduction

The Georgia Division of Family & Children Services (DFCS) outlines detailed expectations for supervised visitation in its Child Welfare Policy Manual, especially under **PAMMS Policy 10.19 (Visitation) and 17.03 (Court-Ordered Contact and Protective Orders).** While these policies are binding on DFCS case managers and contractors, they also serve as best-practice standards for private supervised visitation providers.

By aligning your services with these public-sector expectations, private providers can demonstrate consistency, professionalism, and a child-centered approach that builds trust with courts, attorneys, and families.

Key DFCS Policy Areas & Private Practice Application

1. Timely Initiation of Visitation

DFCS Policy (10.19):

- A face-to-face visit must occur within **7 calendar days of the child's removal** from the home.
- If over 75 miles apart, initial contact must be attempted via phone or video.

Private Practice Application:

Although private providers do not manage removals, timely initiation of visitation following a court order or parent referral mirrors this best practice.

Scenario - Delayed Engagement:

A mother was referred for supervised visitation two weeks after her court date, but due to lack of contact from the private agency, the first visit did not occur until 5 weeks post-hearing. The delay was cited in court as evidence of weak parent-child bond.

☑ Takeaway: Private providers should aim to schedule and initiate services within 7 days of receiving intake applications/payment to mirror DFCS responsiveness.

Key DFCS Policy Areas & Private Practice Application

2. Frequency of Visitation Based on Age

DFCS Policy (10.19):

- For children **0-2 years old**: visitation **at least twice per week.**
- For children **3-5 years old**: **at least once per week.**
- For all others: a **minimum of bi-weekly visits** when reunification is the goal.

Private Practice Application:

Even in high-conflict private cases, these age-based frequencies can guide providers in making recommendations to the court or monitoring case stagnation.

Scenario - Developmental Bonding:

A father visits his 8-month-old son once every three weeks due to his personal schedule. Although he is affectionate, the infant cries throughout each visit.

☑ Takeaway: Explaining the importance of consistent and frequent bonding, especially for infants and toddlers, can help courts order and parents commit to optimal visitation schedules. Recommending
frequency, when court orders do not specify, will be helpful to promote positive outcomes in reunification.

Key DFCS Policy Areas & Private Practice Application

3. Documentation Requirements

DFCS Policy (10.19):

Each visit must be documented in Georgia SHINES within 72 hours.

Includes date, time, interactions, and whether the visit was missed or canceled.

Private Practice Application:

Private providers should establish documentation standards that include timely, factual, and legally defensible observation notes, even when not using SHINES.

Scenario – Court Testimony Discrepancy:

A private supervisor was called to testify in a custody case but had only vague memory and handwritten notes with incomplete dates. The judge gave less weight to the testimony.

✅ Takeaway: Use a consistent format and store reports securely; treat every report as if it could be subpoenaed.

Key DFCS Policy Areas & Private Practice Application

4. Missed and Canceled Visits

DFCS Policy (10.19):

Document any missed visit with reason and attempt to reschedule.

Address patterns of noncompliance in case planning.

Private Practice Application:

Frequent no-shows, late arrivals, or cancellations should be logged clearly. Patterns of behavior can indicate deeper custody or compliance concerns.

Scenario – Manipulation Attempt:

A parent reschedules every visit last minute, then blames the supervisor for "not being flexible." Documentation revealed a pattern that helped the judge assign responsibility.

✅ Takeaway: Detailed attendance logs protect both the provider and the child. Ensure to have a clear policy regarding the booking and cancellations of visits. Stand firm on all contracted agreements to ensure parents understand your "no game-playing" policies.

Key DFCS Policy Areas & Private Practice Application

5. Location and Supervision Level

DFCS Policy (10.19):

Visits should occur in the least restrictive, safe setting: home, community, or agency.

Supervision should adjust as safety improves (e.g., step-down to unsupervised).

Private Practice Application:

Private providers can propose graduated visitation plans that reflect these tiers:

1. Center-based supervision
2. Community-based/off-site supervision
3. In-home supervised
4. Unsupervised transitions

Scenario - Home Visit Resistance:

A parent requested in-home visits right away, but past records showed domestic conflict. The private provider recommended community visits first and outlined a step-down plan for the visiting parent.

☑ Takeaway: Adopting DFCS's progressive visitation model adds structure and clarity to private services.

Key DFCS Policy Areas & Private Practice Application

6. Reunification vs. Restriction Goals

DFCS distinguishes between cases where reunification is the goal versus cases involving **termination of parental rights (TPR)** or long-term guardianship.

Private Practice Application:

Private providers often work in post-TPR or non-reunification settings. Still, framing services with DFCS-aligned goals helps clarify whether the supervision is restorative, investigative, or protective.

Scenario – Misaligned Expectations:

A provider was hired for a parent with a history of abuse. The provider encouraged emotional bonding and increased contact, unaware that the court's goal was to limit visitation.

☑ Takeaway: Providers should always clarify the legal purpose of supervision by obtaining court order: reunification, court compliance, or monitoring parental fitness. Include parents' attorneys, guardian ad litem, and counselor where applicable. Inclusion supports providers in ensuring they are accurately interpreting the court order, parental plan, and/or other legal documents pertaining to the case.

Conclusion

By modeling your private practice after DFCS policies and clearly documenting how your procedures align with or exceed those expectations, you create a practice that is defensible, ethical, and child-centered. Providers who adopt this mindset often receive referrals from attorneys, courts, and even DFCS staff who value consistency and professionalism across sectors.

Chapter 4: Roles & Responsibilities — Public and Private Supervised Visitation Providers

Overview

Supervised visitation involves a collaborative network of professionals working to ensure safe, structured, and emotionally appropriate parenting time. While the Division of Family & Children Services (DFCS) manages the bulk of state-involved child welfare cases, private supervised visitation providers fulfill an essential role in court-ordered, attorney-referred, or family-initiated visitation cases.

This chapter clarifies the core responsibilities of each party involved in supervised visitation and highlights the unique strengths that private providers bring to the process.

4.1 DFCS Case Managers and Public Supervised Visitation

Primary Roles:

- Develop and maintain the case plan and visitation schedule in SHINES.
- Coordinate transportation and location of visits, especially in foster placements.
- Monitor for safety, bonding, and parental progress toward reunification.
- Document each visit within 72 hours.
- Make recommendations to the court based on visitation outcomes and patterns.

Key Characteristics:

- Visits are often scheduled during business hours.
- Facilities may be limited to agency offices or public spaces.
- Staff must adhere to state protocols with limited flexibility.

Strengths:

- Multidisciplinary coordination with schools, therapists, and legal systems.
- Access to full family case history and placement records.

4.2 Private Supervised Visitation Providers

Primary Roles:

- Implement court-ordered or attorney-referred visitation in private custody cases.
- Provide safe, neutral, and trauma-informed spaces for child-parent contact.
- Observe, document, and when needed, redirect interaction in real-time.
- Prepare detailed reports that can be submitted to the court, attorneys, or guardian ad litems.
- Offer flexible options for location, time, and visitation type based on court parameters.

Key Characteristics:

- Operate independently or under business entities (e.g., The Children's Advocate).
- Not bound to DFCS systems, but often mirror DFCS best practices for quality assurance.
- Serve both court-involved and voluntarily engaged families.

Disclaimer: Private providers should never present themselves as working on behalf of DFCS unless formally contracted.

The Unique Value of Private Providers: Personalized, Relationship-Driven Care

Private providers are uniquely positioned to offer a more tailored and consistent experience for families in distress. Unlike public agencies with overwhelming caseloads and limited availability, private providers often:

- Offer evening and weekend hours, accommodating working parents and school-aged children.
- Build rapport with families through consistent scheduling, emotional regulation support, and follow-up guidance.
- Adapt settings to the needs of the child (e.g., quiet parks, supervised home settings, child-friendly indoor spaces).
- Coach parents in real-time (when appropriate), helping them practice better engagement and boundary-setting techniques.

These qualities help restore dignity to the supervised parent and reinforce emotional safety for the child, even under strict legal oversight.

Example – Client-Tailored Scheduling:
A private provider who met with a child on Friday evenings for dinner visits recognized the child was consistently tired and withdrawn after school. By proposing weekend morning visits instead, the provider helped improve bonding and attention between the child and father.

Example – Emotional Presence:
A provider noticed that a mother had difficulty managing transitions when saying goodbye at the end of visits. By introducing a consistent goodbye routine (story + countdown + hug), the provider reduced anxiety and tantrums in both mother and child, ultimately enhancing visitation quality.

4.3 Court Responsibilities in Supervised Visitation

Courts hold the authority to:

- Order supervised visitation and define its terms (e.g., location, type of supervision, duration, transition steps).
- Require specific provider credentials or qualifications.
- Review documentation submitted by DFCS or private providers.
- Approve changes in supervision level (e.g., moving from supervised to unsupervised visitation).
- Evaluate progress and determine whether parenting time should be modified or suspended.

Note: Courts rely heavily on neutral, well-documented reports from both DFCS and private providers in making these decisions.

4.4 Collaboration & Boundaries Between Roles

While DFCS and private providers operate independently, many best practices overlap:

Responsibility	DFCS	Private Providers
Scheduling	Through case manager	Directly with parents or attorneys
Documentation	In SHINES system	In private logs or court templates
Reporting to Court	Through court filings or updates	Through reports or affidavits
Visit Location Flexibility	Limited (office, foster home)	Flexible (home, public, agency office)
After-Hours Availability	Rare	Common
Parent Coaching or Debriefing	Minimal	Often built into the service

Conclusion

Private supervised visitation providers are not simply observers, they are facilitators of healing, accountability, and connection. By maintaining high ethical standards, clear boundaries, and client-focused structure, private professionals play a vital role in Georgia's broader child welfare landscape. When guided by both compassion and legal awareness, private visitation services provide the kind of tailored support that many families need to begin restoring trust and rebuilding safe relationships.

Chapter 5: Visitation Planning & Supervision

Overview

A successful supervised visitation program depends heavily on thoughtful planning, appropriate supervision, and consistency. Whether visits are initiated through DFCS, ordered by a judge, or requested by families in private custody matters, visitation planning must prioritize the child's physical and emotional safety, reflect court expectations, and support the evolving goals of the family.

This chapter outlines the core components of structured visitation planning, supervision strategies, and step-down approaches for transitioning toward unsupervised time when appropriate.

5.1 Components of a Supervised Visitation Plan

A well-developed supervised visitation plan should include:

- Frequency of visits (e.g., once weekly, twice monthly)
- Duration (e.g., 1-hour, 2-hour increments)
- Location (e.g., agency office, home, public space)
- Supervision type (e.g., monitored, therapeutic, interventionist)
- Participant roles (parent, child, supervisor, case manager)
- Prohibited behaviors (e.g., no gifts, no whispering, no discipline)
- Required conditions (e.g., substance testing, therapy completion)
- Documentation and reporting expectations
- Termination or suspension conditions

Private Practice Note: If a formal visitation plan is not provided by the court, private providers should create a written visitation outline and share it with both parties before the first visit. This promotes transparency, reduces conflict, and offers clear boundaries for all involved.

5.2 Scheduling Visits Based on Age and Court Goals

Supervised visitation must reflect the developmental needs of the child and the court's stated objective (e.g., reunification, compliance monitoring, or safety oversight).

Child's Age	**Recommended Frequency**	**Key Considerations**
0-2 years	2-3 times per week	Frequent contact to maintain bonding
3-5 years	1-2 times per week	Play-based interaction; gentle transitions
6-12 years	Weekly or bi-weekly	School-friendly scheduling; social-
13-17 years	Bi-weekly or monthly	Child's comfort and autonomy; structured goals

Court Goal Consideration:

- Reunification = High frequency + consistent progress
- Supervision as a protective measure = Gradual, conditional expansion only if court allows
- Therapeutic reunification = Integrated with counseling, typically slower-paced

5.3 Selecting the Visit Location

Safety, accessibility, and developmental appropriateness should guide location selection:

- Agency or office setting: Controlled, neutral space with supervisor present
- Community-based: Parks, libraries, or family-friendly venues
- Supervised home visits: Transitional setting for reunification cases
- Virtual: Temporary solution if distance, safety, or health risks interfere

Private Practice Tip: Always obtain court or attorney approval before changing visitation settings. Keep a record of parent preferences, child reactions, and any environmental issues (e.g., distractions, weather, conflict risks).

Matching Supervision Style to the Case

Not every family needs the same level of supervision. Considerations include:

- Monitored only: For families rebuilding trust or with minor risks
- Interventionist supervision: For cases with active behavioral concerns
- Therapeutic supervision: For court-ordered trauma recovery or reunification

Scenario – Adjusting Supervision Style:

A provider began with monitored visits but noted that the parent consistently spoke about the other caregiver in front of the child. By shifting to interventionist supervision and documenting this redirective work, the provider helped set clearer boundaries and better prepared the parent for future progress.

Building Predictable Visitation Routines

Children thrive on predictability and preparation. Best practices for structured supervision include:

- Creating rituals for greetings and goodbyes
- Offering sensory or emotional tools (books, calming toys)
- Keeping visits at the same day/time if possible
- Briefly previewing expectations at the start of the visit
- Providing age-appropriate closure ("5 more minutes," "1 more game")

Private Practice Insight: These small routines create emotional safety, especially for children navigating transitions, loss, or reunification fears.

Transitioning Between Levels of Supervision

Progression is key to most visitation plans. The court may approve step-downs if visitation shows consistency, safety, and emotional growth.

Typical transitions include:

- Supervised at agency
- Supervised in community
- Supervised in home
- Unsupervised in community
- Overnight or extended unsupervised visits

Note to Providers: Always consult the court order or referring party before reducing supervision levels. Unauthorized changes, even if well-intended, can jeopardize your credibility or result in liability.

Conclusion

Whether initiated by DFCS or a private provider, visitation planning must be intentional, structured, and flexible enough to meet family needs within court boundaries. Supervisors play a critical role in helping children maintain relationships, observe parental progress, and document patterns that may guide legal outcomes.

Thoughtful planning can be the bridge between supervised oversight and restored family connection.

Chapter 6: Supervision Protocols & Safety Management

Overview

Effective supervision requires more than observation—it involves preparation, clear boundaries, documentation, and structured protocols that ensure every visit supports safety, emotional regulation, and the child's well-being. For private supervised visitation providers, this begins with a professional intake process, a signed service agreement, and consistent safety and response protocols across all visits.

This chapter outlines how to effectively manage intake of visitation supervision clients and safely manage supervised visits while maintaining the professional standards expected by courts, clients, and referring parties.

6.1 Intake Process for Private Providers

Before any visits occur, a structured intake process should be completed to gather essential background, establish legal boundaries, and prepare both parties for the supervised visitation experience.

Step 1: Intake Request & Initial Screening

- Receive intake applications from parents and/or attorneys.
- Contact all parties via email for next steps instructions (e.g intake fees, interview scheduling, document requests)
- Request and review the most recent court order or agreement authorizing supervision, if applicable.
- Screen for basic eligibility (e.g., substance use, protective orders, criminal history, restraining orders, active DFCS cases).

Step 2: Separate Intake Interviews

Conduct individual interviews with each parent/guardian to:

- Review court order terms.
- Review signed supervised visitation agreement/contract.
- Identify risks (violence, mental health, abduction, safety concerns).
- Learn about the child's personality, preferences, and known triggers.
- Establish contact protocols, transportation rules, and drop-off locations.
- Introduce yourself and the process to the child(ren) during the custodial parent's interview.

Private Practice Tip: Avoid joint interviews. Interviews must remain neutral and trauma-informed, prioritizing the child's safety over either parent's agenda.

Step 3: Service Contract & Policies

Both parents must review and sign a Supervised Visitation Agreement, which includes:

- Statement of non-confidentiality (reports may be submitted to court)
- Payment policies and scheduling terms
- Safety protocols (e.g., drug-free visits, no corporal punishment, no whispering or note passing)
- Rules for guests, gifts, and food
- Cancellation and rescheduling terms
- Reporting obligations (to courts, attorneys, or guardian ad litems)
- Emergency procedures

Note: The service agreement also protects the provider legally and sets clear expectations from the start.

6.2 Supervisor Responsibilities During Visits

A professional visitation supervisor is responsible for:

- Monitoring all interactions for safety, appropriateness, and emotional tone.
- Remaining neutral (not taking sides, advising, or engaging in conflict resolution).
- Intervening when:
    - Physical boundaries are crossed
    - Verbal threats or manipulation occur
    - The child becomes visibly distressed
    - A court order is violated

- Documenting facts only (not opinions or diagnoses)
- Ending visits early if risk to the child becomes apparent

6.3 Safety Protocols Before, During, and After Visits

Before Each Visit

- Confirm identity of all parties.
- Ensure transportation has been arranged according to the plan.
- Check that the visiting parent is free of visible impairment (substance use, erratic behavior).
- Remove prohibited items (weapons, bags, recording devices, alcohol).
- Set the tone by reviewing ground rules and expectations.

During the Visit

- Maintain direct visual and auditory contact at all times.
- Avoid distractions (no phone use or side conversations).
- Take notes on parent-child interaction, responsiveness, and redirection needs.
- Remain alert for signs of emotional dysregulation in either party.

After the Visit

- Escort the child to the receiving parent or guardian as scheduled.
- Record any concerns or positive developments in a report.
- Log attendance, timing, and any deviations from plan.
- Provide basic observation checklist/report to all parties prior to visit.
- Communicate with attorneys or courts if reporting is ordered.

6.4 Emergency Procedures and Critical Incidents

Supervisors must be trained to manage the following emergencies:

- Medical event (e.g., asthma attack, seizure): Call 911 and notify both parents.
- Child abuse disclosure: Mandated reporter responsibility—notify DFCS or law enforcement immediately.
- Fight or escalation between parties: End visit, remove child from area, and follow de-escalation plan.
- Violation of court order: Stop the visit and document the violation for court or attorney referral.

Private Practice Consideration: Establish written internal procedures and always have access to emergency contact forms, court orders, and an exit plan for every location

---

6.5 Documentation Standards

Each visit should be documented within 24–72 hours and include:

- Date, time, and duration
- Location and supervisor name
- Parties present
- Summary of interactions
- Interventions or redirections (if any)
- Child's demeanor before, during, and after
- Missed or canceled visit notes, if applicable

Pro Tip: Avoid subjective phrases like "Dad seemed angry", instead write, "Dad raised his voice to child after child refused to sit. Tone was loud and firm."

6.6 Boundaries & Professional Ethics

Supervisors must remain:

- Neutral (no advising or suggesting court outcomes)
- Confidential (except for court-ordered reports or mandated disclosures)
- Professional in all communications with parents and attorneys
- Free from dual relationships (no friendships, romantic relationships, or business conflicts)

Conclusion

A structured intake process, combined with strong supervision protocols and emergency readiness, is what distinguishes a quality supervised visitation provider. Whether operating in the public or private sector, maintaining these professional standards ensures that children experience safe, consistent, and developmentally appropriate contact with their parent—while the provider remains in compliance with legal, ethical, and procedural expectations.

Chapter 7: Compliance with Court-Ordered Conditions

Overview

Supervised visitation exists within the framework of legally binding court orders. These orders define the "if," "how," and "under what conditions" visitation may occur. As a visitation provider—whether DFCS-based or private—you are not only facilitating parenting time; you are enforcing a legal agreement that protects the child's safety and upholds the court's authority.

Failure to comply with these conditions can:

- Jeopardize the child's well-being,
- Place the provider at legal risk, and
- Undermine the credibility of the visitation process.

This chapter outlines how to identify, document, and enforce court-ordered conditions and how to handle noncompliance when it arises.

7.1 Interpreting the Court Order

Before supervision begins, providers must:

- Obtain a copy of the most recent court order
- Highlight or extract all visitation conditions:
    - Dates, times, and frequency
    - Supervision requirements
    - Location limitations
    - Prohibited contact with third parties
    - Program completion (e.g., anger management, FVIP)
    - Substance testing or sobriety conditions
    - Bond or payment obligations
    - Communication limitations (e.g., no discussion of court matters)

Private Practice Tip: Maintain a court-order summary sheet in each client file. You may also request clarification from the referring attorney if conditions are vague or contradictory.

7.2 Substance Use Restrictions

Under O.C.G.A. § 19-9-7, courts may prohibit:

- Alcohol or drug use within 24 hours of a visit
- Visits if the parent appears under the influence
- Visitation unless the parent completes substance use treatment or testing
- Provider Responsibility:
- Visually screen the parent before each visit
- Deny visitation if intoxication is suspected
- Document observations carefully (e.g., odor, slurred speech, imbalance)
- Notify appropriate parties if repeated violations occur

Scenario – Repeated Incidents:
A provider notes that the father consistently smells of alcohol. After three documented incidents, the court pauses visitation and orders inpatient treatment.

☑ **Takeaway:** Enforcing these restrictions protects the child and supports recovery-based court outcomes.

7.3 Conditions for Family Violence Cases

In family violence cases, courts may impose:

- Mandatory supervision (never unsupervised)
- FVIP (Family Violence Intervention Program) completion
- No overnight visits
- No contact with certain individuals (e.g., former partner, siblings)

Provider Note: These cases require heightened vigilance. The child may fear the parent or react to triggers. The supervisor should:

- Review any active TPOs (Temporary Protective Orders)
- Ensure no reference to past violence or litigation is made during visits
- Document any emotional responses, aggression, or boundary testing

---

7.4 Managing Financial Compliance

Some court orders require:

- One parent to pay for supervision costs
- Payments to be made before the visit
- Bond to be posted before visitation begins

Private Practice Considerations:

- Enforce your payment policy consistently—no exceptions without written consent from both parties or the court
- Keep payment records for each visit
- If one parent fails to pay, do not facilitate the visit unless alternate arrangements are ordered

7.5 Behavioral and Environmental Conditions

Courts may order:

- No corporal punishment
- No discussion of court, legal matters, or other caregivers
- No guests at visitation
- No overnight visits
- Confidentiality of the child's or custodial parent's address

Supervisor Actions:

- Remind parties of rules before each visit
- Intervene and redirect when violations occur
- End the visit early if necessary
- Document factual account of what occurred

Scenario – Boundary Violation:

During a visit, a parent begins to show the child court documents and says, "I'm going to win custody soon." The supervisor intervenes and ends the visit.

☑ **Takeaway:** Court-ordered boundaries must be enforced in real time.

7.6 Communication with the Court or Referring Parties

Scenario:

During a supervised visit, the provider observes that the parent repeatedly raises their voice aggressively at the child, uses derogatory language, and makes comments intended to turn the child against the other parent. The child becomes visibly distressed, cries, and withdraws from interaction.

What the Provider Should NOT Do:

- Give legal advice to either parent.
- Make a custody recommendation (e.g., "I think custody should be changed to the other parent").
- Express personal opinions about whether the parent is fit or unfit.

What the Provider Should Do:

Prepare an incident summary using objective, factual language:
Example: "During the visit, at 3:15 p.m., the parent stated, 'Your mom doesn't care about you,' in a loud tone. The child lowered their head, began crying, and moved to the corner of the room. The parent continued speaking loudly for approximately one minute before redirecting to a different topic."

- Report the incident to the court or referring party only if:
  - It involves safety concerns.
  - It reflects noncompliance with court-ordered conditions.
  - The visit was missed or canceled.
  - There is repeated emotional dysregulation or distress observed over time.
- If you are not a mandated court reporter, only share the report when formally requested or subpoenaed.

Private Practice Documentation Tip: Write as if your report will be read in court. Avoid interpretations or conclusions—stick to what was seen and heard. Use date, time, and direct quotes where possible.

7.7 When to Terminate or Pause Services

Visitation may be suspended or terminated if:

- The provider believes the child is in immediate danger
- The parent violates conditions multiple times
- The court or attorney requests a pause

Private providers should notify both parties in writing and refer the case back to the court when:

- A TPO is issued
- Abuse is suspected
- Payment is repeatedly withheld
- Conditions are no longer being met

Conclusion

Supervised visitation must always follow the **letter and spirit of the court order**. As a provider, your role is not only to facilitate time—but to protect trust in the legal process and ensure that visitation serves the best interest of the child.

By strictly enforcing court-ordered conditions, you help maintain fairness, safety, and accountability for all parties involved.

Chapter 8: Training Content & Standards for Providers

Overview

Supervised visitation is a sensitive, high-stakes service. Providers must be prepared to navigate complex family dynamics, manage risk, maintain neutrality, and uphold legal and ethical standards. Whether working with DFCS or operating independently in private practice, providers must undergo training that aligns with Georgia laws, child welfare policies, and court expectations.

This chapter outlines the essential training topics, core competencies, and professional development standards for visitation supervisors across the state.

8.1 Foundational Knowledge Areas

All supervised visitation providers, regardless of their background, should be trained in the following foundational areas:

- Georgia legal framework (O.C.G.A. §19-9-3 and §19-9-7)
- DFCS visitation policies and PAMMS guidelines
- Court orders: structure, enforcement, and boundaries
- Child development and trauma-informed care
- Mandated reporting responsibilities
- Documentation and neutrality in court reports

Note for Private Providers: Because there is no license or degree requirement in Georgia to provide supervised visitation, clear, documented training in these core areas helps establish your credibility and protect you legally.

8.2 Required Topics in Provider Training

A comprehensive training program should include modules or lessons covering:

Topic	Key Learning Points
Legal Compliance	Understanding court orders, prohibited behaviors, interpreting family violence clauses
Trauma-Informed Practices	Recognizing trauma responses in children and parents, responding with empathy
Safety Protocols	Managing emergencies, de-escalation strategies, transport and exchange safety
Neutral Observation	Taking objective notes, avoiding subjective language, avoiding influence on outcomes
Communication Boundaries	Remaining neutral, avoiding dual relationships, professional email and phone etiquette
Reporting & Documentation	Writing court-ready summaries, avoiding bias, documenting redirection
Cultural Competence	Working with families across race, language, disability, religion, and LGBTQ+ identities
Parent Coaching Ethics	When to redirect, how to model without overstepping, staying within scope
Mandated Reporting	When and how to report suspected abuse, neglect, or imminent danger
Privacy & Confidentiality	Understanding what can and cannot be shared and with whom

8.3 Minimum Training Hours and Ongoing Development

Although Georgia does not mandate specific training hours, best practice standards recommend:

- Initial training: At least 12–16 hours before conducting solo visits
- Ongoing professional development: 6–8 hours per year
- Shadowing requirement: New providers should observe at least 3–5 visits with an experienced supervisor

Private Practice Tip: Document every completed training with a certificate, date, instructor name, and content outline in your professional binder or business file.

8.4 Example Training Schedule (Private Providers)

Day 1: Legal & Policy Overview

- Georgia Code: Custody & Visitation
- DFCS policies: PAMMS 10.19 and 17.03
- Reading and interpreting court orders

Day 2: Safety, Supervision & Ethics

- Emergency protocols
- Supervision levels and types
- Professional boundaries

Day 3: Observation, Reporting, and Communication

- Documentation case studies
- Mandated reporting scenarios
- Professional communication strategies

8.5 Ethics, Neutrality & Professionalism

Supervised visitation providers are often the only neutral party in high-conflict family situations. That neutrality must be protected at all times.

Ethical Standards Include:

- No dual roles (e.g., cannot be a friend, counselor, or relative of any party)
- No gifts or favors to/from families
- No recommendations on custody
- No breach of confidentiality (unless legally required)
- Full honesty in court reporting
- Refusing to take cases where bias or conflict exists

Scenario – Ethical Dilemma:

A provider is asked by a parent to "just write something positive" for the judge. The provider politely declines and refers to the neutral documentation policy outlined in the signed agreement.

☑ **Takeaway:** Protect your reputation and service integrity by staying in your lane.

8.6 Certification & Public Perception

In Georgia, there is no centralized certification or licensing body for supervised visitation providers. However, offering clear, written proof of training, insurance, and policy adherence creates a professional standard that courts, attorneys, and parents can trust.

Private Provider Checklist:

- Signed training log or certificate
- Written policies and terms of service
- Contract and intake forms
- Documentation samples or templates
- Business insurance (strongly recommended)
- Clear communication protocols

Conclusion

Training is not optional. It's the foundation of safe, ethical, and professional supervised visitation. By equipping yourself with a full understanding of the law, child behavior, risk response, and reporting, you ensure that every visit supports the court's goals and the child's best interest.

For those in private practice, proper training is what separates "watching a visit" from delivering a legally sound, trauma-informed, court-respected service.

Chapter 9: Reporting, Case Recording & Quality Assurance

Overview

Documentation is one of the most powerful tools a supervised visitation provider has. It informs court decisions, reinforces safety, and provides an ongoing record of parent-child interactions. Whether you're contracted through DFCS or operating independently, accurate, neutral, and timely documentation is essential for credibility, legal protection, and the child's well-being.

This chapter outlines best practices for documenting supervised visits, managing case records, and maintaining internal quality assurance.

9.1 The Role of Documentation in Supervised Visitation

Supervised visitation records can be used to:

- Inform attorneys, judges, and guardians ad litem
- Monitor compliance with court orders
- Support or dispute custody modification requests
- Identify trends in parenting behavior and child response
- Protect the provider from legal liability

Note: Any record you create may be subpoenaed. Write with the assumption that judges, attorneys, and parties may read your notes aloud in court.

9.2 What to Document After Each Visit

A standard visit report should include:

- Date, time, and duration
- Names of all participants
- Visit location
- Arrival and departure times
- Observations of parent-child interaction
- Supervisor interventions (if any)
- Child's emotional state (before, during, after)
- Compliance with court conditions (e.g., sobriety, no guests, no gifts)
- Missed or canceled visits (including reasons)

Avoid these documentation pitfalls:

- Using judgmental language (e.g., "Mom was hostile")
- Assuming motives (e.g., "Dad was trying to manipulate the child")
- Diagnosing (e.g., "The child has anxiety")

☑ Instead, write:

"Mother raised her voice when child refused to sit. Child turned away and began to cry. Supervisor intervened to redirect and offer a toy."

9.3 Documentation Formats

Private providers may choose from several formats:

- Narrative Reports (paragraph-style summaries)
- Checklist Forms (structured for consistency)
- Hybrid Forms (short answers with room for notes)

Choose a format that:

- Is consistent
- Meets legal or attorney expectations
- Can be stored and retrieved securely

Private Practice Tip: Develop a template branded with your business name and include a footer with date/time and supervisor signature.

9.4 Frequency and Timing of Reports

DFCS caseworkers must submit visit notes into SHINES within 72 hours

Private providers should complete documentation within 24–72 hours of each visit

- Ongoing Documentation Includes:
- Progress summaries (e.g., monthly, bi-weekly)
- Incident reports (as needed)
- Termination or discharge summaries

Delayed documentation risks memory gaps, reduced credibility, and potential liability.

9.5 Handling Missed, Canceled, or Disrupted Visits

Always document:

- Who canceled (parent, provider, child, court)
- When the cancellation occurred (e.g., same-day, 24 hours in advance)
- Whether it was excused or not (e.g., medical emergency vs. no show)
- Attempts to reschedule
- Patterns of attendance or inconsistency

Scenario – Court Review of Attendance:

A mother's attorney claimed she attended every visit. The provider's logs showed three no-shows and two cancellations in the last six weeks.

☑ **Takeaway:** Accurate records protect the supervisor and provide clarity to the court.

9.6 Quality Assurance (QA) Practices for Private Providers

Even in solo or small-team practices, quality assurance should be built in. Suggestions:

- **Monthly case review**: Re-read all reports for completeness and clarity
- **Check for bias**: Review language and consistency across families
- **Use a checklist**: Ensure that each report contains required elements
- **Audit feedback**: If working with attorneys or courts, request structured feedback on your reports

Pro Tip: Save redacted examples of strong reports as internal training tools or future staff templates.

9.7 Record Storage & Confidentiality

Maintain records in compliance with:

- **Georgia record retention expectations** (generally 3–5 years for court-related documents)
- **HIPAA or FERPA**, if applicable to your professional role (e.g., licensed mental health provider)
- **Mandated reporting requirements** if abuse is disclosed or suspected

Secure Storage Options:

- Password-protected digital files (cloud or local drive)
- Locked filing cabinets (for hard copies)
- Dual access logs if multiple providers share cases

Conclusion

Documentation is more than an administrative task, it's your professional voice. By producing clean, neutral, and complete records, you ensure transparency, reduce conflict, and support healthy legal outcomes. Strong documentation is one of the most compelling tools a supervisor can offer the courts and families they serve.

Chapter 10: Resources & Appendices

Overview

To ensure this training manual is not only educational but practical, this chapter includes tools and reference materials that supervisors, particularly in private practice, can use immediately. From sample forms to legal summaries, these appendices support the consistent, lawful, and trauma-informed delivery of supervised visitation services across Georgia.

Appendices

Appendix A: Sample Georgia Visitation Plan Template

This sample visitation plan can be adapted for both court-referred and voluntary private cases.

It includes:

- Names of parties and children involved
- Type of visitation (monitored, therapeutic, etc.)
- Location and supervision level
- Frequency, time, and duration
- Arrival and departure procedures
- Rules for conduct (no corporal punishment, no derogatory remarks, no gift-giving, etc.)
- Conditions and limitations (e.g., no substance use 24 hrs prior)
- Emergency contacts and supervisor responsibilities

☑ **Use this template to structure client intake and create clarity for all involved parties. Many times clients will come with court approved visitation/parenting plans within their court-orders.**

Appendix B: Sample Court Order Language

This appendix provides sample language courts may use (or you may encounter) in visitation-related orders, such as:

- "All visitation shall be supervised by a neutral third-party approved by the court."
- "Supervised visits are to occur no less than twice per week for two hours per visit."
- "The supervised parent shall not speak negatively about the other parent in the presence of the child."
- "No other parties shall be present during the visit except the court-approved supervisor."
- "The visitation provider shall submit a written summary every 30 days, or immediately upon incident."

☑ **Private providers can use this as a reference to confirm compliance or to request clarification from attorneys.**

Appendix C: DFCS Policy Highlights — PAMMS 10.19 & 17.03

Summarized key points from DFCS visitation policy:

PAMMS 10.19 – Visitation Standards

- Minimum visitation frequencies by age
- Importance of bonding and emotional connection
- Requirements for first visit within 7 days of removal
- Scheduling standards for foster care and reunification cases
- Visitation plan development and updates in Georgia SHINES

PAMMS 17.03 – Court-Ordered Contact

- Supervisory protocols when protective orders exist
- DFCS coordination with external providers
- Court authority on visitation limitations

☑ **These highlights help private providers align with public standards and enhance court trust.**

Appendix D: Summary of Georgia Statutes & Case Law

O.C.G.A. §19-9-3 – Best Interest Factors

- Emotional ties
- Capacity to care for the child
- Criminal history and substance use
- Child's preferences (11+ may be considered; 14+ presumed)

O.C.G.A. §19-9-7 – Supervised Visitation Provisions

- Conditions for visitation involving violence or abuse
- Program requirements (e.g., FVIP)
- Legal authority for supervision and suspension

Illustrative Case Examples:

- *Smith v. Smith*, 2021: Court upheld supervised visitation where child expressed anxiety during transitions and therapist supported monitoring.

- *In re K.J.*, 2020: Visitation denied due to repeated noncompliance with court-ordered supervision.

☑ **Use these statutes to educate clients and protect your role as a lawful facilitator, not a decision-maker.**

Appendix E: Monitor Code of Conduct

As a visitation monitor, I agree to:

1. Maintain professionalism at all times and treat all parties respectfully.
2. Adhere strictly to all confidentiality requirements, sharing information only with authorized parties.
3. Remain neutral and avoid favoritism, bias, or personal involvement with any party.
4. Follow all safety and emergency response protocols outlined in the training manual.
5. Document visits accurately, factually, and in a timely manner, without personal opinion or judgment.
6. Enforce all court orders and visitation agreements as written.
7. Avoid any conflicts of interest and report any potential conflicts immediately.
8. Refrain from engaging in personal, business, or social relationships with clients outside of scheduled visits.
9. Report any violations, safety concerns, or incidents according to established procedures.
10. Acknowledge that failure to follow this Code of Conduct may result in removal from the visitation monitor roster and/or legal consequences.

☐ **I acknowledge that I have read, understand, and agree to the above Monitor Code of Conduct.**

Printed Name: ___________________________

Signature: _______________________________

Date: _____________

References

Bowen, M. (1978). Family therapy in clinical practice. Jason Aronson.

Bowlby, J. (1982). Attachment and loss: Vol. 1. Attachment (2nd ed.). Basic Books.

Bretherton, I. (1992). The origins of attachment theory: John Bowlby and Mary Ainsworth. Developmental Psychology, 28(5), 759-775.

Department of Human Services. (n.d.). Child welfare policy manual: PAMMS 10.19 - Visitation. Division of Family & Children Services. https://pamms.dhs.ga.gov/dfcs/cws/10-19/

Georgia Department of Human Services. (n.d.). Child welfare policy manual: PAMMS 17.03 - Court-Ordered Contact. Division of Family & Children Services. https://pamms.dhs.ga.gov/dfcs/cws/17-03/

Justia US Law. (n.d.). O.C.G.A. § 19-9-3 - Custody and visitation; best interest of the child. https://law.justia.com/codes/georgia/2020/title-19/chapter-9/section-19-9-3/

Justia US Law. (n.d.). O.C.G.A. § 19-9-7 - Visitation in cases involving family violence. https://law.justia.com/codes/georgia/2020/title-19/chapter-9/section-19-9-7/

References

Samuel Thomas Law. (n.d.). Supervised visitation in Georgia. https://samuelthomaslaw.com/supervised-visitation-in-georgia/

Sharon Jackson Attorney at Law. (n.d.). Supervised visitation in Georgia child custody cases. https://sharonjacksonattorney.com/supervised-visitation-in-georgia-child-custody/

Siegel, D. J., & Bryson, T. P. (2012). The whole-brain child. Delacorte Press.

Stearns-Montgomery & Proctor. (n.d.). Know the guidelines and rights for supervised visitation in Georgia. https://stearns-law.com/child-custody/know-the-guidelines-and-rights-for-supervised-visitation-in-georgia/

Substance Abuse and Mental Health Services Administration. (2014). SAMHSA's concept of trauma and guidance for a trauma-informed approach (HHS Publication No. SMA 14-4884). https://ncsacw.samhsa.gov/userfiles/files/SAMHSA_Trauma.pdf

Tervalon, M., & Murray-García, J. (1998). Cultural humility versus cultural competence: A critical distinction in defining physician training outcomes in multicultural education. *Journal of Health Care for the Poor and Underserved*, *9*(2), 117-125.

WomensLaw.org. (n.d.). Custody and visitation in Georgia. https://www.womenslaw.org/laws/ga/custody

🔹 Continue Your Journey with The Children's Advocate

🎓 Live Supervised Visitation Trainings

Take your knowledge beyond the manual!

Join Dr. Arkeria S. Wright for live, in-depth training sessions designed to help private and public providers master the art of safe, ethical, and legally sound supervised visitation.

These trainings are perfect for:

- New professionals launching a private practice
- DFCS caseworkers and contractors
- Attorneys and family court professionals seeking insight into best practices
- Anyone pursuing supervised visitation certification or professional development hours

👉 **Training Topics Include:**

- Intake & interview protocols
- Georgia family law & DFCS policies
- Safety management in high-risk cases
- Documentation & court testimony
- Trauma-informed and culturally responsive supervision

📚 Access More Digital Resources

Get downloadable tools, templates, and professional development guides that support your ongoing learning and business growth.

📌 Visitation forms & sample contracts
📌 Digital workbooks & supervisor toolkits
📌 Certificate templates and intake checklists
📌 Specialized resources for private practice

🔗 Start Learning Today

💻 Visit: https://thechildrensadvocate.com/professional-trainings
📩 For group bookings or licensing inquiries, contact:
info@thechildrensadvocate.com

Special Feature – About The Children's Advocate & Our Book

The Children's Advocate is dedicated to empowering families, protecting children, and equipping professionals with the tools to provide safe, effective, and compassionate supervised visitation services. Founded by Dr. Arkeria S. Wright, our work blends advocacy, education, and heart.

Don't miss Dr. Wright's inspiring book, Advocating for Children with Love — a guide for becoming an advocate for children both professionally and personally. Available now on Amazon, this book offers real-world strategies, heartfelt stories, and expert advice to help you make a difference.

Because every visit matters. Every child deserves safety. And every advocate deserves the right tools to lead with love.

Shareables

The Children's Advocate
SPECIAL EDUCATION ADVOCACY
SUPERVISED VISITATION
ADVOCATING FOR CHILDREN WITH LOVE
TO BE SEEN. TO BE HEARD.
TO BE LOVED.
ADVOCATING FOR CHILDREN WITH LOVE
678-829-2355
INFO@THECHILDRENSADVOCATE.COM
VISIT WWW.THECHILDRENSADVOCATE.COM TO LEARN
MORE ABOUT THE BENEFIT OF OUR SERVICES

The Children's Advocate
SPECIAL EDUCATION ADVOCACY
SUPERVISED VISITATION
ADVOCATING FOR CHILDREN WITH LOVE
TO BE SEEN. TO BE HEARD.
TO BE LOVED.
ADVOCATING FOR CHILDREN WITH LOVE
678-829-2355
INFO@THECHILDRENSADVOCATE.COM
VISIT WWW.THECHILDRENSADVOCATE.COM TO LEARN
MORE ABOUT THE BENEFIT OF OUR SERVICES

The Children's Advocate™

ISBN 979-8-9997813-0-7

9 798999 781307 >

www.ingramcontent.com/pod-product-compliance
Ingram Content Group UK Ltd.
Pitfield, Milton Keynes, MK11 3LW, UK
UKHW060019051026
15591UKWH00003B/277